GHOST SOJOURN

Ghost Sojourn

Gwen Sayers

SOUTHWORD*editions*

First published in 2024
by Southword Editions
The Munster Literature Centre
Frank O'Connor House, 84 Douglas Street
Cork, Ireland

Set in Adobe Caslon 12pt

ISBN 978-1-915573-11-7

Contents

In Transit *7*

Notes from a Centaur's Curator *8*

Simulacra *9*

Graveyard Shift *10*

Walls *11*

Double Exposure *12*

Listening to Holst *Mars* while watching Bellator MMA on TV *13*

A Forest Witch Passes *14*

Drop Dead Beauty *15*

Last Paso Doble *16*

Heirloom *17*

The Ripple Effect of Locusts *18*

The Wake *19*

We Don't Understand Why *20*

Inbox *22*

RIP *23*

Archbishop Tutu's funeral seen from thousands of miles away *24*

Riptide *25*

Acknowledgements *26*

In Transit

My father fled the morgue on New Year's Eve, two days
before we buried him. He travelled with the north wind,
spitting sleet. He blew in through a keyhole with his fogged
mind, clogged heart, and homelessness. The house shivered.
I turned up the thermostat. An iridescent scarab clattered
across the floor and vanished under the sofa. I poured Scotch
on the rocks, set the glass by the couch, played him a lost
violin concerto. He sobbed. At night, his shade propped
against the door frame. I followed his sighs to the living room,
watched pixels blur as he surfed the box. I turned the TV
off. He turned it on again. He sent me blank texts, flashed
the phone's red light, emailed links to ancient Egyptian rites.
His welterweight scars and smashed teeth never bothered
me. Neither did his astral technology. I missed him when he
slipped away in March.

Notes from a Centaur's Curator

Lift the dust cover, gently. The centaur
is old, in bits, you may lose some.

His hooves paw straw in a glass case.
They kick. Comb the feathering with care.

Ears share a drawer with jet eyes
and a warped arrow. Use a damp sponge.

He still calls from his voice box
for Scotch on the rocks. Ignore.

Braid his white tail in a chunky plait,
truss the chaos with ropes to secure.

Rub his freckled back, curry his sides,
soothe the scar on his neck with lanolin.

When you polish his knuckles, forget
your bruises. They're safe in the chest

with dead ends, nightmares and shadows
he fought. Air out these memories

and fold away. Replace his musty shroud.
Turn off the lights when you leave.

He is happiest in the dark.

SIMULACRA

I was six
when I shifted a curtain
    in a dark room
at the waxwork museum
and peered through glass
    at a woman

I remember
    hooks and chains
    her tattered skirts
    pale lips
crimson stains

I thought of her
first time I lifted
    black tarpaulin
    exposed a sallow man
his wrinkled skin
puckered face
closed eyes
    all of him sweated formalin

I remember the incision
    that opening up
his bloodless vessels
inert nerves
those Latin names
    I never remembered

Graveyard Shift

On call in a rundown hospital,
I find a bed, climb steel sides,
sprawl on a rubber mattress.
A manager binds my limbs

with shreds, stands at the beside,
casts a long shadow over me,
swings his two-faced stethoscope
like a lasso above my head.

He taps a Camel on the ball
of his hand, flicks a Zippo,
blows a kiss. Toothed leaves
gnaw on moonlit windows.

A matron thumps a keyboard, pumps
a pedal while a wounded centaur
gallops in circles, drumming triplet
rhythms on the concrete floor.

The door swings open. Granddad,
who cries from only one eye,
limps into the ward wheeling
his tin hat on a rattling trolley.

When dawn crows, the matron,
injured centaur, my grandfather,
and the manager, goosestep
out of the door into the day.

WALLS

mice run upon the walls
an infant gurgles in a cot
clouds whirl above

outside these walls
wisteria swings purple
blooms within the walls

a tomcat leaps
spits blood under the rug
mice twitch in a corner

between these walls
you dance with me behind
this wall we kiss

below a moon tree
I dream inside the walls
lose a ring plant dill

on window sills against
this wall branches
crackle smoke curls

bats fly above this wall
shadows sleep
deep beneath the walls

Double Exposure

I'm boxed in between Bert and
Albie on a bench at a trestle table.
The garden ahead, with its sundial,
bird coop, and red hot pokers,
climbs towards a brick wall.

Albie inches his arm closer,
my skin tingles. I glance
at his bushy eyebrows, long lashes,
thatched lip. He clears his throat,
offers me an empty laboratory.

Bert grabs my hand, shares
his dreams of formulae, his
Mahler playlist. The sun pitches in,
blinding me. Halos of hair
glisten around both men's heads.

I slide closer to Albie, his familiar
emptiness, aromatic aroma.
I want to be with Albie, work with Bert,
be with Bert, work with Albie.
Draw a straw. Flip a coin. Throw dice.

Is Albie long or short? Is Bert
heads or tails, high or low? While
I draw, flip, shake and throw,
both ghosts fade into my pile
of failed mergers.

LISTENING TO HOLST *MARS* WHILE WATCHING BELLATOR MMA* ON TV

Distant footfall. My father leaves work, brooding, choked by mezzo ideas. He warms up, stokes his rage. Imperial Blue searchlights slice the Bellator Stadium. Crowds bay for Pitbull. Shoulders sway. Umber daze. Bellator. Minotaur. Matador. Ork. Punches crash. Pewter. Steel. Brass. Dissonance. Pitbull in the red corner bares his gum guard. Sizes up his opponent's inkings. Faces down in the high pitched, wire-mesh cage with a bone white, blood-smeared floor. Cymbals clash, scarlet as a low kick. Arms swing, fists thud. Muscles bulge, feet drum. Pitbull's jabs blaze maroon edged with indigo. My sullen father unlocks his car. Cracks his knuckles. Revs. Pulls out of the car park. Limoges Blue shatters. Pitbull takes down, grounds and pounds. The smell of sweat, fear, and rust percuss the stadium. *Protect yourself at all times.*

*Mixed Martial Arts

13

A Forest Witch Passes

After Paul Klee: *Forest Witches*

their mother
       is cushioned
       in moss
pillowed by mud
& falling apart

prehnite eyes hover
over cursing tongues
woodlice crawl
       below
       black teats
branches creak above
       gilled hearts
       clawed toes

she sprawls
among runes
       blood stains
       copper sheets
spilled gall
& toad foam

she offers a gift
       to her progeny
neon-pink pomegranate
lodging toxic worms

her son pours colour
       down her throat
& taps his foot

DROP DEAD BEAUTY

I'm scrolling the news feed thinking about how exquisite my mother was, when I see a wicker coffin that looks like a hamper with rope handles down the sides. My mother shades her eyes, their picnic basket contains remains of eggs, sausage and lipstick. My father spies behind a lens, steals her blood red lips, black curls and yellow basket in a snapshot. He never managed to pry open her casket – *a tisket, a tasket*. Not with kisses. Not with fists. If he had, he would not have found her secret letter. My grandmother used to visit them with a basket of meat pies. She wasn't afraid of wolves. The natural woven coffins on my screen are made of willow, seagrass, cane, and wicker; all pictured against scenic beauty. A lake at sunset. A field of bluebells. A forest path. You can click on a colour or type of weave that suits you. Choosing a coffin online is like buying a sofa. The sofa can have an ash or pine frame. Grey or green fabric. Soft or firm cushions. A wooden casket can be lined with silk or satin. Its handles, gold or silver finished. And didn't e. e. cummings ask Mister Death how he liked his blue-eyed boy? In the end, we have no choice. That's the beauty of it.

Last Paso Doble

My mother clatters up, twirls sunset skirts,
extends her femur, offers brittle metacarpals.
Castanets snap, guitars twang, tambourines rattle.

Listen, it's our music, she says. *Time to dance.*
I'm the matador and you're the bull.

She thumps her heel in dust. Paces towards me.
Teeth chatter. Knees crack. Carpals clang on her pelvis.
I know her voice, recognise the music,

step aside. *Let's face it, Mum,*
skeletons can't lead.

Her skull pivots, eye sockets search.
She swivels. Her hands reach, vertebrae collapse.
I leave forget-me-nots at her grave.

HEIRLOOM

A book, borrowed by my mother
from her friend Sylvie, passed on
so I could cook Millicent's fish dish.

Did I say my mother died
during lockdown? So I can't, couldn't

It's her writing on the blank pages
that gets me. Her left handed, backward slant.
Rita's Osso Bucco, Vera's pea soup.

Musty, cookbook, colour of lightly toasted
pine nuts. I cough, reading the index.
My eyes burn. I try, but can't

Dark stuff, sauce, maybe gravy,
stains her words. After death she can't.
Couldn't. No one takes things back then.

What she wrote is all I have

armour-plated locusts, olive and brown. Speckled wings, jagged legs, exoskeletons. Collisions. Their mandibles, jaws, eating disorders. And cockroaches, fat landlocked prawns crawling in underwear drawers. Flying ants, biplanes, drones. Drones with cameras. Those with black eyes, compound eyes, green eyes, blind eyes. Insects that crackle, rattle, scuttle, bang on windows, force their way in. Under doors. Through cracks. Holes in floors. Locusts on bookshelves, cicadas behind blinds. The Amazon. Lepidoptera. Giant Neuroptera. Praying Mantis. Prayers. Revelation. Chapter 9. The horses, faces, teeth, hair, wings, power. Locusts, crucified on grilles, yellow blood spattered on windscreens. Large moths bumping on panes. Stick insects, pick-up-sticks, angled legs, protractors, geometry. Back legs knotted in my hair, scratching my arms. Daddy-long-legs, sugar daddies, promiscuous daddies. Flying, diving, planes, helicopters, hang gliders, parachutes. Clicks in the dark. Therapists. Desensitization. Visualization. Locust in the corridor. In this room. On my chair. On my shoulder.

THE WAKE

Frantic pecking on the front door
woke me. Emperor penguins
jammed the hall; heads bowed,
gold-tinged bellies, backs coated black
in morning suits.

My father, grandmother, grandfather
and aunt clasped bouquets
under their wings; white lilies
wrapped in cellophane. The smell
of iceberg clung to them.

They shifted flat feet, peered sideways
with obsidian eyes, and shuffled
soundlessly to the living room.
I lifted the weightless birds
onto the sofa, one by one,

piled frozen peas and fish fingers
in a Pyrex dish, poured iced water
into wine glasses. But, by the time
I got back from the kitchen,
my penguins had melted.

We Don't Understand Why

One tectonic plate slid over another
below the Indian Ocean and in Cape Town
your granddad who never cried,
howled in his sleep.

A ripple reared. Raced towards beaches
where palm trees rustled and bathers'
oiled bodies gleamed on the sand.
You lay there.

On Boxing Day, a flagpole fell
on your granny's head at a funeral.
Stunned, she asked repeatedly:
What happened?

In Jo'burg, your tabby leapt six feet,
impaled its body on a spiked
metal fence. *Not normal behaviour
for a cat,* said the vet.

In Somerset, your mother's alarm
went off, unset, and shrilled
until she removed the battery.
Something is broken, she thought.

In London, your aunt's candles dipped.
They flickered and smoked
as match after match licked their wicks.
The room lost its twinkle.

In Sydney, your cousin, aged nine,
threw a bottle into the tide. The letter
inside asked the sea to return you.
Waves ebbed, left beaded streaks.

We found you in Krabi, ten days later,
wrapped like the others in pitiful rows.
Your navel ring, your long blonde hair,
unchanged.

Inbox

Your email, sent at midnight to my turned-off screen,
travelled with bats' wings, moonbeams, bark of an urban fox.

I want (in bold black font) to die (Arial 16 point) peacefully
in my sleep. A woman bandaged in ivy trailed over
desolate ruins in my dreams.

I opened your message at nine, after grinding coffee,
cracking eggs, burning toast. Your bold black font, large print,
shuddered on my screen. Magnetic letters pattern the fridge.

Nobody gets clichés. I phoned. My question stuttered
in voicemail. My texts stalled in a void.

I still tended tears from the time you parked underground,
below those pigeons perched on pipes; that day you climbed
pissed-on stairs, trudged through dark corridors
to say goodbye on the third floor. While you were up there,
the birds in the garage flapped aimlessly between metal ducts.

RIP

darkscape   empty moon   scrape a plectrum
hear it scream   *have a good day*
pluck   discords   crack   mirrors

there's room   on the moon   for peppermint crisp
green chartreuse   menthol rings

cryopreserved mammoth tusks
ribs shed   in the wake   of glacial retreat
breathe on ice
thaw amber specks   of dna   trapped in
tufts of wool

you knew they'd take   time   to find you
in the garage   curled up
     in a freezer

ARCHBISHOP TUTU'S FUNERAL SEEN FROM THOUSANDS OF MILES AWAY

white carnations tied with string wilt on Tutu's
coffin. cheap pine, like my old bed in Cape Town. the
strangeness of unbelonging. London under sombre skies.
they say his ashes will be interred below flagstones in St
George's. tyres burn and flames cremate in Gugulethu.
a mourner fans her masked face. memories unfurl. how
Tutu quells a mob, saves a life. Thabo Makgoba swings
a censer over the coffin. after the service, aquamation.
liberation. a nation's pain soaked in hot water. Mama
Leah Tutu sags in a wheelchair under the weight of
purple. her daughter says, *thank you Daddy for teaching me
to love.* our father teaches me to fear. fear of locusts, tidal
waves and quicksand. the white-robed choir sing Nkosi
Sikelela. a south-easter unsettles palm trees opposite the
cathedral. my father covers half his face with a spade-
like hand, plays the piano with his other. faster, faster,
phantom of the living room. the bronze bust of Tutu
looks on. when did he teach his daughter? after work.
after swigging two whiskeys, my dad says, *the haa-de-dah
ibis in our garden carries souls of the dead.* I believe him.

Riptide

I was looking for shells,
driftwood, sea urchins,
cuttlebones and shrimp
in the swash zone

when I found you
ambling on pocked sand,
splashing through strands
of glistening foam.

We strolled hand in hand
to the end of the beach
where a jetty fractures
the swell. I left you

behind like a sandcastle
for kids to knock down,
waves to wash away,
a full moon to freeze.

Although I've forgotten
the colour of your eyes,
the sound of your voice,
the scent of your skin,

you're with me each time
I walk on hard sand,
taste salt on my lips,
feel the tide bathe my eyes.

Acknowledgements

Thanks are due to the editors of the following magazines and anthology in which some of these poems, or earlier versions, first appeared. *Acumen, DMQ Review, Dream Catcher, Ink Sweat & Tears, Magma*, Nine Pens *Hair Raising Anthology, Obsessed with Pipework, Orbis, Right Hand Pointing, Tears in the Fence*, and *Unbroken Journal*.

"Archbishop Tutu's funeral seen from thousands of miles away" was awarded First Prize by Marvin Thompson in the Magma Poetry Competition 21/22.

Gratitude to David Caddy and Louise Buchler for mentoring my work, to my Poetry School teachers, to Alonna Shaw for our poetry exchange, and to my friends at Herga Poets.

Finally, huge thanks to Norman and Greg, readers over my shoulder, for their love and support.

Printed in Great Britain
by Amazon